A Gift of
TIME

A Gift of TIME

FINDING
DYNAMIC PURPOSE
IN RETIREMENT

BOB LITTLE *with Bill Schillings*

A Gift of Time: Finding Dynamic Purpose in Retirement

Copyright © 2024 by Nancy Little

First paperback edition 2024

ISBN 979-8-9903600-2-0 (paperback)
ISBN 979-8-9903600-3-7 (eBook)

ACKNOWLEDGMENT

This book would not be in your hands without the dedication, hard work, and many hours of creativity on the part of Bill Schillings. When Bob placed all his research and the outline of the book into Bill's hands, I know Bill had no idea what he was getting into. I also know that God had a plan; it was to see Bob's vision come to fruition. I cannot begin to express my sincere gratitude for the many hours that Bill put into this project. I will be eternally grateful to Bill and his wife, Liz, for walking beside me during this process.

—Nancy Little

TABLE OF CONTENTS

FOREWORD

After sixty-two years of marriage, I thought I knew everything there was to know about Bob Little. But as it turned out, he didn't always tell me *everything*. After we had settled into our retirement, I noticed Bob was spending a lot of time on the computer. Bob had an accounting background, and financial management was a passion for him. I assumed he was spending all that time researching investments. He would often emerge from his office and make comments like "We now have enough money to live to be 105," or "I just sold some stock and made $125."

Also, I noticed Bob always perked up around friends who shared his interest in investing.

Even though I rarely followed much of these financial discussions, I was happy for him. It was a great hobby with a tangible purpose, and Bob loved it. However, I still couldn't understand why he needed to spend so much time in front of the computer. It surprised me to find out that while Bob was sequestered in his office overseeing our finances, he was also researching and writing a book on biblical retirement.

Throughout our retirement years, I noticed that many people sought Bob's advice on navigating the transition from full-time work to retirement. Bob read widely about biblical principles for retirement, and he found it sad that so many people struggled in that phase of life. We had leadership roles with a group of retirees at our church, so I figured his interest was also because of our involvement there. It wasn't until he began talking with his friend Bill Schillings that I realized maybe something more was going on.

When Bob was diagnosed with cancer in the spring of 2021, our whole world shifted. We became totally engaged with doctor's appointments, treatments, surgery, and medicine. This continued into the beginning of 2022. Bill and his wife, Liz, were part of a group of friends that surrounded us with encouragement and support. During this time, Bob asked Bill if he'd be willing to pick up the pieces of a book he'd started on biblical retirement. Bill agreed, and after meeting together several times, Bob handed over all his files, notes, and research articles. This book is the result of that collaboration . . . with a little support from me.

I think it gave Bob a sense of peace knowing that this book would find its way into your hands after he was gone. If you are approaching retirement or are already living out that season of life, I would highly recommend using the principles in this book as a guide. They provided the framework through which Bob and I lived out a happy and fulfilling retirement.

—Nancy Little

PREFACE

Life is made up of moments, small glittering pieces of mica in a long stretch of gray cement . . . knowledge of our own mortality is the greatest gift God ever gives us.
—Anna Quindlen

*A*s a pastor, I have had the privilege of officiating and attending many funerals. I have been present when families had to make difficult decisions regarding the lives of their loved ones. I've seen retirees decline both physically and mentally and, conversely, seen them face health and death issues triumphantly.

Throughout our retirement years, my wife, Nancy, and I have frequently been asked perplexing questions about retirement. We have two sons, and retirement will be upon them faster than they may realize. My conviction is that God would have me, as well as my wife, model to those around us, particularly our family, what it means to grow old gracefully and face death with realistic optimism despite declining physical and mental abilities. We have a passion to convey this optimism through the practice of biblical living. This book is the result of my research and observations on this topic. And my desire to share some of the principles Nancy and I have found helpful.

As we get older, it's easy to tell ourselves, "I've worked hard, I've done my part, and now I deserve to just look after me during this closing chapter of life and enjoy the rewards life has denied me before. I'm finally free to do my thing. I've done my part—now I'll have fun!" We tend to have lots of excuses for being self-centered as the years fly by.

We set up our little idol and call it "My Golden Years." We assume we have the right to do our own thing, to reap the benefits of whatever we've laid up. We think we deserve it. It's not selfish, it's simply fair. But let's be sure our "now's my chance" attitude has God in the center of it. We must decide: Are we going to invest in these years or waste them?

If God is not the priority, we may travel, recreate, play golf, spend hours in front of the TV—and end up unfulfilled. On the other hand, arthritis or cancer or Alzheimer's may abruptly cut off our glorious plans, leaving us full of bitterness in our last days.

As I looked at Psalm 73, I saw that the psalmist allowed himself to envy the strong and prosperous who went their own way. He wondered if he'd lived a pure life in vain, and his heart became grieved and bitter. Then God reminded him that the highest thing life can offer is His presence, His direction, and the wonder of having Him hold our hand, guide us, and promise to take us to glory. The psalmist responded: "Earth has nothing I desire besides you. My flesh and my heart may fail, but God is the strength of my heart and my portion forever . . . As for me, it is good to be near God. I have made the Sovereign Lord my refuge; I will tell of all your deeds" (Psalm 73:25–28).

Challenge yourself to be prepared to give something new to others through God's life in you. Pray for others to have an ever-growing faith in God's promises. Ask God to let His beauty shine through you and draw *others to Himself. Embrace whatever the future may hold as an opportunity to love others more and grow ever closer to your Savior.*

Look past the false worldly values that surround us. When faced with challenges, refuse to harp on how bad things have become. Nurture a keen enjoyment of both the new and the old. Keep your heart and mind open to your value in God's eyes at any age, in any culture, and in any circumstance. Be an example to those who are younger to help them absorb realities about God that will enable them to find their way in today's world.

Finally, plan time for fun and take a trip occasionally, but keep it all in perspective. The higher goal is to spend time with God. Remember that He has a purpose for you in retirement.

Bob Little intended to use those words to introduce a book he was working on about retirement. Unfortunately, he passed away in June 2022 before completing it. What follows here is the story of how his book came to be. But before we go there, maybe a few words about Bob would be helpful.

In April 2022, Bob's doctor told him that he had about two months to live, as nothing more would counter the effect of the cancer that had invaded his body. Bob and his wife greeted the news with a sense of relief, gratitude, and hope (you'll understand more about how that was possible as you read more about Bob). Thankfully, during that short window of time, Bob was weak but not in much pain, and his mind was, for the most part, still sharp. Those moments

with Bob took on a new significance for his family and friends, because time takes on a different meaning when you're in the presence of someone who has so little time left. You tend to listen more carefully, hear more clearly, think less about yourself, and appreciate life in deeper ways.

As I sat down to write the rest of this Preface, an excellent book by David Brooks called *The Road to Character* came to mind. In it, Brooks talks about the difference between résumé virtues and eulogy virtues: "The résumé virtues are the ones you list on your résumé, the skills that you bring to the job market and that contribute to external success. The eulogy virtues are deeper. They're the virtues that get talked about at your funeral, the ones that exist at the core of your being—whether you are kind, brave, honest, faithful; what kind of relationships you formed." So, in introducing Bob, I thought the résumé/eulogy dichotomy might be a good place to begin.

Bob was born in December of 1939 and raised in Philadelphia, Pennsylvania. He graduated from Frankford High school in

1957, served in the Air Force from 1960–1964, and graduated from Temple University in 1970 (after thirteen years of night school). Bob, an entrepreneur at heart, moved to Charlotte, North Carolina, to start a distributorship for industrial lifting equipment in December of 1971.

After concluding Charlotte was the right place to build his business and raise his two boys, he moved his family there in June 1972. Bob's business acumen, sales skills, and work ethic led to success through the 1970s and '80s. In 1980, he was elected chairman of the elder board at a small, Evangelical Free church called Church at Charlotte. Three years later, during a time of turmoil at the church, Bob was asked to take a full-time position as the associate pastor. Since that meant he'd need to leave his thriving business, this would require a leap of faith. But after a long walk on the beach with his wife, Nancy, they decided that God was calling him to be a pastor. Although, to put it in Bob's words, "I was not called to the pastorate, I was called to Church at Charlotte."

He left the existing business in Nancy's hands until their customers could find other suppliers, anticipating that the business wouldn't survive more than five years. However, that business lasted another twenty-plus years and provided for Bob's family in ways they never anticipated.

Meanwhile, Bob partnered with Jimmy Kallam as Church at Charlotte grew. Jimmy became the lead teacher and senior pastor, while Bob oversaw the business and administrative details as executive pastor. In 2004, at age sixty-five, Bob retired from the church after serving there for twenty-four years. Although, as Nancy reports, "He didn't retire well." Bob was restless in retirement—he still had a passion to serve, loved a fresh challenge, and exuded plenty of energy. Bob had been serving on the board of directors at Hope Cancer Ministries in Charlotte for a number of years. In 2005, they asked him to become their executive director. This position enabled him to continue using his gifts to serve others before transitioning into full retirement in 2011.

It's uncomfortable for me to summarize Bob in this way for two reasons. First, the résumé is so lacking regarding who Bob was at the *core of his being*. Second, the word *retired* has connotations in our society that didn't apply to Bob—more about this later. The résumé virtues don't do much when it comes to describing who a person really was—how they impacted their world, the relationships they formed, their ability to live for a purpose beyond themselves.

To truly define a person, we must turn to the eulogy virtues . . . and in Bob's case, those were plentiful. If pressed to select just one, I'd choose the word *love*. Love for God, love for "my Nancy" (as he referred to his wife), love for his family, and love for his friends (I've been blessed to be in this last category). Now, he would be the first to admit he wasn't perfect, and I know that's true. However, I can't think of anyone who exemplified the biblical imperative to "love God" and "love others" more than Bob Little. And, to my mind, that is a pretty big deal.

Another word that comes to mind is *equanimity*— "mental calmness, composure, and evenness of temper, especially in a difficult situation," according to my Google search. Bob simply exuded equanimity: He and Nancy had a type of peace and contentment that's hard to describe. Bob knew there were people who wondered whether he fully understood the implications of his prognosis and why his attitude seemed so full of hope. He didn't quite grasp this himself, even though he knew where it came from. I heard him comment multiple times that "I realize my situation, but I don't think I'm delusional." I think that will make sense as you learn more about Bob. He was genuinely filled with gratitude for the gift of time with his wife, family, and friends—to laugh, to cry, to talk, and to plan. During one of our final conversations, Bob said, "Of the sixty-two years of marriage to Nancy, this is the best time of all." Now that's something that makes you think.

Bob called this posture of living "realistic optimism," a term he learned from a woman with ovarian cancer during his days with Hope Cancer Ministries. As he quietly eased into his last days, he told me that one of the first things he prayed each morning was, "This is the day that the Lord has made, and I will . . . damn it . . . make the most of it." He was not happy about losing his voice, about growing weaker by the day, or about knowing that his Nancy was suffering as well.

But up to this point in my life, I've never seen a better example of how acceptance leads to serenity, suffering to blessing, and trust to peace. What a blessing; what a gift. Bob made the choice to live well until he died, and he knew that God was giving him the power to do that . . . he knew this didn't come from him alone.

Bob had been working on this book about retirement for many years. This was not only because of his life experience, but also due to his exposure to others who seemed to be struggling with that stage of life. Over time, he shared with me some of the major themes, many of which I found profound, but as he got sicker, progress on the book became slower. As Bob weakened, I figured I had better visit him to find out the status of the project. By this time, unfortunately, he no longer had the energy or interest to work on the book. I thought, *Bob has all these good thoughts about retirement stored up somewhere, and they're going to be lost?* This was not good. I wanted to read his book, and I figured a few other people would feel the same.

Thinking that maybe I could help bring his book to fruition, I asked Bob if he'd be willing to let me look at what he had. He (kind of) hopped out of his chair, clutched his walker, and meandered into his office. I followed closely behind to guard against him falling. For the next thirty minutes, he was lost in front of his computer, totally focused. His printer started to spit out papers. I thought that maybe I'd stop him to ask if I could simply copy the files. *Nah, better just let him do his thing.* When he finished, he also gathered the file full of articles related to retirement that he'd pulled off the internet. "Here, take this too," he said. As if he were mentally checking the box in his head called "Retirement Book." He knew he had gone as far as he could. Finally, he looked me in the eye and told me how grateful he was that his book might be completed after he was gone. And off I went.

When I got home and spread his material out on my dining room table, I felt a bit overwhelmed. The papers contained many great ideas, but it was all a bit disjointed, some of it was redundant, and much of the book simply wasn't written yet. Bob had told me those parts were "still in my head." I did my best to figure out how to organize the book, but I quickly came to a standstill.

I called Nancy—she was Bob's personal secretary those days—to ask if I could come over to see him again. I figured I could ask Bob directly how to organize the book and flesh out his ideas. Fortunately, I recorded that conversation, because by this time, Bob's mind was getting, as he put it, "foggy." He went on tangents often, but as he spoke, I could sense God's presence. I wished we could have talked the whole evening. That hour was a gift—full of stories, biblical concepts, and deep insights. The next day, I spent a few hours transcribing what Bob had said. I realized then that he hadn't been going on tangents after all. He was simply communicating on a different level—one you arrive at when you start to disconnect from this world and get closer to the next. I wound up listening to that recording many times before this project was finished.

I tell you all this because in the purely technical sense, this book hasn't been written by Bob. I've taken what he wrote on the topic of retirement, pieced it together from what I gleaned in conversation with him, and filled in the gaps to the best of my ability. My hope is that it captures the essence of Bob's spirit and reflects his way of thinking.

The stage of life we call retirement has relevance for us all, both individually and communally. I think you'll find Bob's perspective on the topic thought-provoking, insightful, and full of hope.

May the good Lord, and Bob's spirit, be with all of us as we absorb Bob's wisdom.

—Bill Schillings

INTRODUCTION

Do not conform to the pattern of this world, but be transformed by the renewing of your mind. Then you will be able to test and approve what God's will is—his good, pleasing, and perfect will.
—Romans 12:2

I read a story recently that really hit home. It was about a successful salesman named Chuck who was summoned to the home office of the company for which he worked. He assumed he would be congratulated for surpassing his quota and awarded a substantial bonus check. Instead, they told him the corporation was making some changes and he was no longer needed, though they offered a lucrative severance package. Since he was slightly past retirement age, Chuck felt good about the transition to a new lifestyle. He looked at retirement as an exciting new adventure in which life would be carefree and fun.

But Chuck loved his job. He had developed friendships with many of his customers and built a strong community among his coworkers. During his working years, Chuck could best be described as trustworthy, kind, and smart—the kind of person you always enjoyed seeing. He lived a successful life: married to his wife of forty-plus years, enjoying the "empty nest," and enthralled with being a grand-parent. He and his wife, Patsy, had accu-mulated a healthy retirement savings.

Unfortunately, Chuck changed during his retirement. He started to constantly complain about all his aches and pains; he often bragged about his great career and how wonderful life had been then. In time, he lost his ability to listen (often interrupt-ing others in the middle of their sentence) and grumbled about everything. In short, he became a person to avoid.

When Chuck had announced his retire-ment, he assumed Patsy would likewise change her lifestyle. It never entered his mind that she might not be ready for retirement. Patsy's mind was flooded with questions and concerns. She resented that Chuck assumed she would give up her job and join him in retirement. Prior to the arrival of their children, Patsy had enjoyed a fulfilling teaching career. While raising her children, she kept teaching as an occasional substitute teacher. When the kids were grown and out of the house, she took a position as a teacher's assistant. Patsy loved her life and resisted changing it. However, as she witnessed Chuck's change in behavior, she decided that maybe it would be better if she also retired. It was a big mistake. Before long, she began to be irritable, particularly with Chuck. He was always talking about nothing, complained a lot, and didn't help around the house . . . the list seemed endless. He simply wasn't the same man.

Chuck's retirement was so abrupt that he and Patsy had no time to process, plan, or anticipate the changes it would bring. And Chuck quickly discovered that watching television, taking trips to the gym, and looking for ways to fill his time were leaving him feeling empty. He was physically deteriorating, emotionally distraught, and lonely. Some have described Chuck's situation as "work withdrawal," and for Chuck, it was becoming deadly.

The last thing I wanted to do was to replicate the mistakes Chuck had made in failing to plan for his retirement.

SEARCHING FOR ANSWERS

I've often wondered why retirement can bring so many challenges. After all, in our society people usually associate retirement with rest, contentment, travel, playing with the grandchildren, and other leisure activities. We don't expect it to bring about emotional and physical reactions that cause so much stress. I think one reason for this is because retirement can represent a loss of many things—identity, relationships, steady income, activity, vitality, and structure. You can try to deny these losses and sink into depression, or you can choose to accept them. Psychology tells us that a sense of loss usually leads to some form of anxiety. Loss forces us to deal with change. And life in retirement is all about change. Most of us do not like change.

I have enjoyed an eclectic career with many new opportunities and challenges, most of which involved dealing with changes that I handled well. However, as I have grown older, I've noticed that I resist change more. I seem to gravitate toward a comfortable routine that has often led to a feeling of boredom with a touch of fear.

As I approached retirement, I realized I had conflicting emotions that were all based around fear. Financial fears about investments, inflation, budgeting, and so on. Relational fears about how spending more time around the house would affect my relationship with my wife. Identity fears about having no vocation that gave me a sense of purpose. But the nature of fear is that it is almost always illusory. I knew that God had never before let me go hungry; my wife and I had a long history of a healthy, growing relationship; and I was convinced that my identity rested in God's love for me.

When I first started thinking of retirement, many different topics required consideration. What would day-to-day life look like? What would fill my time? How would Nancy and I integrate our separate lives into a cohesive pattern? How long would retirement last? Would there be enough money for the rest of our lives? So, Nancy and I started planning.

We planned three trips over three months immediately after my official retirement to establish a break in our routine. We temporarily discharged all our responsibilities for those three months. During that time away, we discussed what our lives would look like from there on out. This was a joint discussion that included my interests, Nancy's interests, and our common interests. We then set some priorities and discussed how to work it all into our new lifestyle.

Since we had always been involved in our church and almost all our friends were connected to the church, we decided to get involved with something completely different from church ministry. Nancy and

I had always enjoyed the performing arts. For years, we had held season tickets to the performing arts center. This expense was not in our retirement budget. However, when we went to performances, we noticed there were volunteer ushers. We learned that by volunteering, we could see all the shows we wanted, without paying admission. This was a win-win situation and a great example of how planning paid off in our retirement years.

Nevertheless, as I began my retirement, some big questions still spun around in my mind: Who am I? Where am I going? How am I going to get there? I didn't necessarily have the answers to those questions. I did, however, have some clarity about my purpose. I believed that it was to focus on modeling two things, primarily for my children and grandchildren: *how to grow old gracefully* and *how to die well*. The big question was how to do it.

CULTURAL VS. BIBLICAL RETIREMENT

Around this time, I came across an article that laid out the cultural or secular view of five stages of retirement. As I thought about these stages, they didn't leave me feeling inspired to move into retirement with any enthusiasm or purpose. Here was the basic idea:

1. Honeymoon: early period of high spending, travel, and checking off the bucket list, followed by anxiety as the uncertainty of retirement settles in.

2. Practical Planning: big decisions about *where* to live, *what* to do with our free time, *who* to be, and *how* to pay for it all.

3. Static Purpose: inordinate focus on "self"—our accomplishments, our challenges, our pleasures, our money, our families, and so on. (There's nothing wrong with

paying some attention to these things; the issue is one of priority.)

4. Loss/Loneliness: health, cognitive abilities, and mobility all start to decline. During this stage, we begin to lose loved ones that have played a significant role in our lives.

5. Death: the end of life as we know or understand it—a final ending. Awareness that the great unknown is approaching leaves us uncertain and anxious.

Looking at that list left me with a feeling of despair. Where was the hope? Where was the purpose and meaning? Where was the chance to make a difference? In the strictest sense, retirement could simply be defined as when you stop working to earn a living—when income accumulation stops and paycheck withdrawal starts. To my mind, that definition left much to be desired.

As a Christian, I just couldn't believe I had no purpose beyond myself in my retirement years.

I just couldn't believe I had no purpose beyond myself in my retirement years.

On the contrary, I hoped these years might prove to be not only satisfying but also meaningful. I wanted to face the experience of growing old with realistic optimism. I could choose to give in to a life of despair as I looked at a downward spiral from Honeymoon to Death. Instead, I could gratefully focus on the reality that I had been given the gift of time to make a difference, continue to grow, establish new relationships, enjoy God's creation, and love others better.

So, as I thought about how I could best live out my purpose in retirement, I came up with alternative stages of retirement that reflect the biblical, God-centered worldview I've tried to live out my whole life. This paradigm represents an opportunity to contribute to the world and to those we love, while living with purpose and hope. This book describes what, I believe, is a better way to think about retirement. It's organized according to what I call the Seasons of Retirement:

1. New Beginning

2. Purposeful Planning

3. Dynamic Purpose

4. God's Provision

5. New Home

My hope is that you find encouragement in the following pages. But most of all, I hope that viewing retirement in this new way brings you closer to God's presence and purpose in your life.

CHAPTER 1

NEW BEGINNING

*Therefore, if anyone is in Christ, a new creation
has come: The old has gone, the new is here!*
—2 Corinthians 5:17

Life without a paycheck is a new beginning. It's the end of one phase *and* the start of another. The people who struggle most are often those who've had retirement forced on them or those who haven't put much thought into planning for this stage in their lives. It's at this point that you must make a choice: Will you wallow in bitterness and despair, or will you seek meaning and purpose, regardless of your circumstances?

The key step is to decide where (or to whom) you will look for guidance. For me, God's words provided the basis for how I approached this new beginning. The truths and promises from Psalm 118 sank into my soul:

When hard pressed, I cried to the Lord; he brought me into a spacious place . . . The Lord is with me; I will not be afraid . . . The Lord is with me; he is my helper . . . It is better to take refuge in the Lord than to trust in humans . . . The Lord is my strength . . . The Lord's right hand has done mighty things! . . . This is the day that the Lord has made; let us rejoice and be glad in it.

The psalm begins and ends with the same statement: "Give thanks

*to the Lord, for he is good; his love
endures forever."*

I made three conclusions about retirement as I meditated on those verses. First, I needed to *remember how God has been with me in the past.* One of the blessings of age is that I've had so many more experiences of God's goodness. Each day, I carry with me the memory of the many times, both good and bad, when I've experienced the presence of God in my life.

As Jacob was dying, he gathered his children and grandchildren around him to bless them, proclaiming that God had been "my shepherd all my life to this day" (Gen 48:15b). The basis for his blessing and the joy of his "retirement" was in being able to recall all the ways God had seen him through. One example of that in my life was when I returned to Philadelphia after serving four years in the Air Force. I got a job, Nancy and I bought a house, we settled into a church, and then I went back to college. We had two sons by this time, and it was a very busy time in our lives.

My career was moving along and on the surface all was well. But an unsettled feeling took root in my soul. My restlessness led to a desire to start my own business. As I pursued that vision, one open door led to another and I ended up moving our family to Charlotte, North Carolina. That was the best decision I ever made. Looking back, I know, like Jacob, that this was God's leading. My shepherd has indeed been with me all my life.

Second, retirement is best viewed as a time to *appreciate the blessings given by God right now.* I can't do all the things I used to do in my younger days. I can't keep up with my grandkids. I miss a lot of words in conversation. I'm not making money like I used to. However, I continue to be blessed with new experiences that wouldn't have been possible before I retired. For example, for many years Nancy and I lived on a lake just outside of Charlotte. We loved living near the water and having the flexibility in our schedules that retirement provided. But the greatest blessings invariably came from the relation-ships we built with our family and friends at our lake house. Material things don't mean much unless you can share them with others. I know that God is providing that opportunity where I live now as I cultivate a spirit of gratitude for His blessings each new day.

The third conclusion I made as I reflected on Psalm 118 was that retirement provides the opportunity to *trust in His provision for the future*. Because God has been my helper in the past, I know I can trust Him to direct my future. The truth of God's Word means that I can look forward to God guiding me throughout my retirement years and eventually into life in His kingdom after my time on earth concludes.

This way of looking at life is what Charles Spurgeon called the "rule of three" in his book *The Power of Prayer in a Believer's Life* (based on 2 Corinthians 1:10 and Hebrews 13:8). Spurgeon wrote, "Whatever our circumstances are, however perplexing our pathway may be, and however dark our horizon, if we argue by the rule of 'He has, He does, He will,' our comfort can never be destroyed."

A friend once told me that he hated retirement. I knew the only real comfort I could offer would be in directing him toward a "God-centric" worldview based on the rule of three. After some discussion, we concluded that it wasn't retirement he hated, it was old age and, at a deeper level, the prospect of death. But I reminded my friend that for the Christian, death has no sting. He had no need to worry, because Christ has given each believer victory over death.

Considering that reality, the real question becomes, will we be able to face sickness, diminished abilities, and the loss of loved ones in a way that will bring glory to God? We don't know what tomorrow will bring, but we can be encouraged knowing that the Lord will always be with us, just as He has been in the past. "The rule of three" enables us to face each new day as an opportunity to rejoice. This, I knew, was a paradigm shift for my friend (and maybe for you, too), but it's one that represents good news of hope and meaning in our retirement years.

RICHNESS TOWARD GOD

As I continued to think about how to approach retirement, I was convicted by the parable of the rich fool and Jesus's teaching about worry in Luke 12:13–31:

Someone in the crowd said to him, "Teacher, tell my brother to divide the inheritance with me."

Jesus replied, "Man, who appointed me a judge or an arbiter between you?" Then he said to them, "Watch out! Be on your guard against all kinds of greed; a man's life does not consist in an abundance of possessions."

And he told them this parable: "The ground of a certain rich man yielded an abundant harvest. He thought to himself, 'What shall I do? I have no place to store my crops.'

"Then he said, 'This is what I'll do. I will tear down my barns and build bigger ones, and there I will store my surplus grain. And I'll say to myself, "You have plenty of grain laid up for many years. Take life easy; eat, drink, and be merry."'

"But God said to him, 'You fool! This very night your life will be demanded from you. Then who will get what you have prepared for yourself?'

"This is how it will be with whoever stores up things for themselves but is not rich toward God."

The rich fool, in response to having stored up plenty of "good things" for many years, decides to take life easy—eat, drink, and be merry. God calls him a fool whose "life will be demanded" from him that night. The plans he had made to live a self-centered life of luxury would therefore be meaningless. When Jesus told His story of the rich fool, He was responding to a concern. Two brothers were having a disagreement about the family inheritance. Jesus told them to be wary of the temptation to be greedy. Then, notice that the story itself only has one person in it—the rich fool. Nothing is said about his workers. When the rich man considers his options, he speaks to himself and no one else. One of the problems with greed is that we only consider ourselves and not those around us.

Richness toward God must include a consideration and *love of others*. 1 Corinthians 13 speaks eloquently about this. It says that being rich toward God is a lifestyle that is patient, kind, rejoices in truth, always trusts, always hopes, and always perseveres. A person rich toward God does not boast, is not proud, is not self-seeking, is not easily angered, keeps no record of wrongs, and does not delight in evil. For the Christian, the new beginning of Scriptural retirement is simply a continuation of a Christ-centered life. It's based on relationships and the promise of a new home (more on that in chapter five).

Richness toward God also involves trust. Upon finishing His parable about the rich fool, Jesus went on to teach His disciples not to be anxious about their basic survival needs (food, clothing, and so on). He said, "Therefore I tell you, do not worry about your life, what you will eat; or about your body, what you will wear . . . For the pagan world runs after all such things, and your Father knows that you need them. But seek first his kingdom, and these things will be given to you as well." We are being called to trust God with a force greater than our fears—a trust that counters our anxieties and compels us to rely on God for everything.

So, the questions for me became: Could I be rich toward God regardless of how much money I had stored up? Could God's commands be viewed as a recipe for richness toward God? Could I demonstrate this richness to the people within my circle of influence? As I understood the Bible, the answers were a resounding YES.

My conclusion was that richness toward God relates to two things: loving others and trusting Him. Therefore, those elements should guide my thinking about the new beginning of retirement.

DEALING WITH REGRET

However, as I looked at that list from 1 Corinthians 13, I became overwhelmed. As I endeavored to love the Lord with all my heart and to love my neighbor as myself, I realized that I often fell short. I wish I could tell you that I've been rich toward God in all my ways. I have not. I'm often poor in trusting God, loving Him, and loving others. I often do that which I should not do and don't do what I know I should (Romans 7:14–20). But in the face of regret, I often think of a quote attributed to C. S. Lewis: "You can't go back and change the beginning, but you can start where you are and change the ending."

I needed help to change the ending, and I believed help would come from the Lord as I depended on Him for strength and guidance. I needed His grace to free me from the sin of not being rich toward Him 100 percent of the time. I needed His wisdom as I set the goals found in Scripture and rested upon His will to mold me into the image of His Son.

I once knew a grandfather who confided in me with great lament, "I have been a horrible father. I should have never had children." I knew him and his family. I had to admit he had a point—he hadn't been too successful as a family man. The sad thing was that he now believed that all was hopeless.

This man had just retired.

I proposed that his retirement was an opportunity for a new beginning. And with some encouragement, he started to pour his life into his six grandchildren. Basketball games became one of his favorite pastimes with the boys, and the girls liked going out for dinners with Granddad at their special restaurants. He found himself truly enjoying those moments with his grandkids. Withdrawing from work gave him the opportunity to find richness toward

God along with purpose in a place he hadn't expected. Not only did this minister to his grandchildren, but it also showed his children that with God's help, he had the capacity to change the ending of his life.

Even though we may have failed in the past, God's love and grace will prevail—if we stay open to His leading and the opportunities that retirement provides. The new-beginning phase opens a window of opportunity in which we can better seek God's will and wisdom. Retirement frees us from the pressures of maintaining a career and the intensity of the child-raising years. It allows us to integrate the aging process with the gift of time.

The new-beginning phase opens a window of opportunity in which we can better seek God's will and wisdom.

Understanding and implementing this philosophy can sometimes be challenging. Fortunately, we aren't left to do it on our own. In Ephesians 3:20, we read that God can do "immeasurably more than all we ask or imagine, according to His power that is at work within us." With this power, we can invest in God's command to make disciples and love others more intentionally. We can enjoy a growing relationship with God as we find joy in His creation—and learn from one another as we plan for the time we have left.

CHAPTER 2

PURPOSEFUL PLANNING

Commit to the Lord whatever you do,
and he will establish your plans.
—Proverbs 16:3

When I was eleven, my parents told me that I had to start helping the family by getting a job. They would take care of my laundry, as well as provide meals and a roof over my head. All other expenses, present and future, were my responsibility—school supplies, clothes, car, college education, and so on. I know by today's standards that may seem harsh. But in the early fifties, it was more of the norm. My closest friends and many of the other kids in our blue-collar neighborhood also worked after-school jobs. In my case, the timing was good—my older brother had a job delivering newspapers and was going into the Navy, so I just took over his paper route.

I would like to tell you that I managed my money well. Unfortunately, even though I did work hard, that wasn't the case. I doubled my paper route, painted the porch railings for some neighbors, and returned used soda bottles to make extra income. I loved having my own money . . . but I also loved spending it. At that point in my life, I considered saving money a waste. In my youthful arrogance, I believed I could always get a job and make more money.

Six weeks after my seventeenth birthday, I graduated from high school. The only goals my friends and I had were to secure the best jobs we could find and buy a car. Sure enough, within a few months, we had all managed to achieve those goals. My car was a red and white Chevy Bel Air. The only thing left on the agenda, before being drafted into the military, was to have a good time and start looking for a girl to marry. Planning for a career and a future was not part of my mindset.

Fortunately, I had a big brother who was my hero. His approval was very important to me. That summer, he and his wife came by to show me his brand-new car, an Olds '88 two-door hard-top. In our neighborhood, if you had a Chevy, Ford, or Plymouth, you were doing well. An Oldsmobile was a bigger deal.

He sat me down on the front step, pointed proudly to his new car, and said, "Would you like to have a car like that someday?"

"Yeah, yeah," I answered.

"Would you like to maybe buy a new car every three years?"

Again, I nodded.

"Would you like to someday marry and buy a nice house in the suburbs?"

Again, my answer was yes.

"If that's what you want," he said, "you're going to have to go to college! Here's the phone number to call to set up your entrance exam to Temple University night school. You're good at math. Go for a business degree and major in accounting."

I can't put into words how impactful that conversation with my brother was. At the time, I had no vision for the future, and what he told me was beyond my comprehension. However, the plan made sense and came from someone I respected. I followed his advice and enrolled at Temple, which laid the groundwork for a lifetime of professional and financial success that set me up to retire many years later.

It all started with a vision followed by a plan for action—thanks to my brother.

VISION, PLANNING, AND WILLINGNESS TO ACT

For fifty-four years, I built on the work habits of my youth and the vision my brother had laid out for me. Since I had started working when I was eleven, by the time retirement came around, it was obviously a change in every aspect of my life.

As I looked back on what God had blessed me with, I saw a life of material blessings and people I loved. This filled me with much gratitude. But I must admit that after more than a half-century of income accumulation, losing the security of a paycheck provoked an enormous amount of anxiety within me.

So many practical questions needed to be addressed:

- Will Social Security survive?
- How long will my wife and I live?
- Will we have enough money?
- How will we manage our investments?
- What Medicare plan do I choose?
- Should I have long-term care insurance?

The questions seemed endless.

The transition from working (income accumulation) to the potential of twenty or thirty years of unemployment (paycheck withdrawal) can be scary. So, from a practical standpoint, I knew I needed three things: a vision for success, a plan, and the willingness to act on that plan. If you don't have those three ingredients, you'll never be able to retire successfully.

My parents were good examples of this. When they retired, Dad wanted to relax and spend time helping others. Mother wanted to invest their money and leave her sons an inheritance. At one point they moved to Charlotte to be near our family. We had bought a home that needed a lot of work. Dad was always available for any project that required his help. Mother kept her nose to the grindstone with her investments. Both my parents saw the fulfillment of their visions individually. But they also wanted to travel together to see parts of the country they had never visited while earning a paycheck. They blended their individual and corporate visions, planned well, and acted accordingly.

Years later, I used their example in my own retirement. Nancy and I had started a tradition of taking a family vacation every year because time with our family was important to us both. As the family grew, we needed to rent a bigger and more expensive house for these trips. We believed that this should continue to be a priority, even though we realized it might stretch our retirement budget. This was a step of faith, but we were willing to trust God with that decision. It's amazing how much trust goes into the willingness to act. For us, it was a way of "seeking first His kingdom and not worrying about tomorrow" (Matthew 6:33–34). We budgeted for that trip every year, and it was the best investment we ever made.

The plan for success will flow naturally out of your vision. If you want to check things off your bucket list, you must first look at your finances and budget wisely. You can't travel the world and then be unable to afford fixing the roof on your house. Fruitful planning must balance the practical, recreational, and unexpected variables of your life. It's about making thoughtful and wise decisions. For instance, while I spent a lot of my time researching stocks and investing our money, Nancy had an opportunity to work a part-time job. Since the job was flexible and didn't interfere with our retirement plans, Nancy worked for a number of years to earn extra money.

So many of my actions before retirement were based on a continuing flow of income. My actions post-retirement needed to be considered relative to our savings and how long those finances would last. It's a different mindset that requires a balance of trust in God's provision for the future while wisely using the resources that He has entrusted to us today. Even though God doesn't promise us tomorrow, we have a responsibility to plan for it just the same.

HOLDING PLANS LOOSELY

I knew the practical aspects of retirement were important, but the question I thought about most was: What is to be my purpose in retirement? As I mentioned earlier, I decided my purpose was to model for my kids and grandkids how to grow old gracefully and die well. For guidance in that arena, I always looked to biblical principles and God's direction—thankfully, I didn't have to look far.

For any Christian, the biblical injunction is to strive to be "more like Christ." I realize the meaning and implications of that term might be challenging. We can spend a lifetime trying to figure this out, let alone trying to do it. This, I think, is part of God's intention. It motivates us to constantly rely on Him and seek His presence—particularly when we don't have all the answers. For me, one thing was clear. Jesus clearly lived an "others-centered" life. He was all about serving others and living for a purpose beyond Himself. I knew that somehow, some way, I was to follow that example in my retirement. I needed to focus most on using whatever God had blessed me with to bless others. Retirement wasn't meant to be all about me!

Some Bible verses came to mind. The first was, "Trust in the Lord with all your heart and lean not on your own understanding; in all your ways submit to him, and he will make your paths straight" (Proverbs 3:5–6). My desire to have a biblical worldview in retirement dictated that this be a core principle. It gave me great comfort knowing that I could fully trust God with the direction, specifics, and results of my life in retirement. I didn't need to rely solely on my abilities (what a relief). I didn't need to understand what He was doing every step of the way. I simply needed to trust that God would direct and guide me. The rest was on a need-to-know basis. Sometimes what I think I need to know and what God thinks I need to know can be two different things.

Another passage that provided great insight was Jesus's advice about worrying in Matthew 6:25–34. Specifically, Jesus talks about what not to worry about, including: your life, what you will eat or drink, your body, what you will wear, or what will happen tomorrow. Unfortunately, when I thought about many of the retired people I knew—and my own inclinations—I realized that practically everything we worried about was on that list. Clearly, the biblical perspective presented a more reasonable and practical foundation for retirement.

I needed to focus most on using whatever God had blessed me with to bless others. Retirement wasn't meant to be all about me!

Lastly, I considered the following verse: "And whatever you do, whether in word or deed, do it all in the name of the Lord Jesus" (Colossians 3:17). Based on your spiritual perspective, that may sound either brilliant or baffling. For me, it simply meant that I needed to be mindful of the reality that everything in my life was "from Him and through Him and for Him" (Romans 11:36). My life in retirement needed to be a grateful response to God's provision for me, filled with faith that I could entrust God with my future.

After reading these verses, I realized that while planning was a necessity, I needed to hold my plans loosely. My part was to surrender to Him, follow His direction, and rely on His help. Only God knew what I needed to see, who I needed to be, and what I needed to do. Therefore, I needed to focus on His purpose and will for my life, wherever they led me. The practical concerns were simply a part of that purpose—the means to an end, not the end in itself.

CHAPTER 3

DYNAMIC PURPOSE

*My grace is sufficient for you, for my
power is made perfect in weakness.*
—2 Corinthians 12:9

Building a career and raising children automatically gives us purpose during our "working" years. The passing of these stages generates a void. I once knew a Christian couple who exemplified this. Their focus in retirement was traveling extensively. They had time and resources but, unfortunately, never seemed fulfilled. They were living in denial about their lack of purpose. They were also running from the reality of death. Death is inevitable, but from a Christian perspective, it's not something to be feared. Put into the proper eternal perspective, death is precisely what serves to bring meaning to our remaining time on earth. In that sense, death is to be embraced. There's nothing inherently wrong with vacations, unless they cause folks to miss out on the peace of mind, purpose, and richness of life that's found in having an eternal, Christ-centered worldview.

As I was approaching retirement age, I felt I could no longer perform my job at the highest level. The timing was right for me to move on. As I mentioned earlier, it was at this point that Nancy and I took three months off and enjoyed some time away. The purpose was to prayerfully assess what changes needed to be made in order for us to have a graceful and meaningful retirement.

During those three months, we checked off many items on our bucket list: we traveled, tried new things, and generally had lots of fun just being together. And we still do. But we often had a nagging question, Is this all there is? I think that's because, without a higher purpose, checking items off a bucket list is more about what we get than what we give. This usually leaves us feeling hollow and disillusioned.

As our three-month hiatus ended, I realized that I missed working. I liked being productive, achieving goals, and being around people. However, I also liked the flexibility of not working a full-time job. I struggled with this tradeoff for some time. Then I was offered a part-time position that would provide a perfect transition period. To my surprise, that job lasted for seven years. It gave me the opportunity to feel useful and ease into a full retirement. Finally, when that job grew into more of a burden than a blessing, it was obvious to me that I was ready to fully retire.

Around this time, I searched the Bible for direction and guidance. I came upon an Old Testament passage that I found inter-esting. In Numbers 8:25, the Lord declares the following about Levite men: "At the age of fifty, they must retire from their regular service and work no longer." This seemed to validate my decision to stop working altogether.

However, as a result of taking some courses at a nearby Bible college, I remembered one of my professors saying that when you quote Scripture, you should include its context. So, I went back to Numbers 8 and noticed that verse 26 states that the retired workers "may assist their brothers in performing their duties." Technically speaking, the retired Levite men weren't working, but they still played an important role in assisting others. Older folks were to *retire from* something but *retire to* something else. As I sought out what that might be in my case, this biblical perspective provided insight and motivated me to keep reading the Bible.

THE ONE ANOTHERS

One thing became crystal clear; Scripture is a book about relationships . . .

with God and with our fellow man. For me this was best expressed by Jesus after washing His disciples' feet in John 13:34–35, when He said, "A new command I give you: Love *one another*. As I have loved you, so you must love *one another*. By this everyone will know that you are my disciples, if you love *one another*" (italics mine).

The New Testament refers to the "one anothers" quite often. Obviously, then, our relationships with other people are of paramount importance. As I sought vision for a purposeful retirement, I knew I needed to *retire to* a life based on the "one anothers" found in Scripture. To understand this better, I organized verses involving the concept of *one another* and *each other* into six categories: love, acceptance, encour- agement, caring, affection, and instruction. Here are just some of the examples:

LOVE

- "Greater love has no one than this: to lay down one's life for *one's friends.*" —John 15:13

- "Let us love *one another*, for love comes from God. —1 John 4:7

- "Since God so loved us, we also ought to love *one another*."
  —1 John 4:11

- "Let no debt remain outstanding, except the continuing debt to love *one another*." —Romans 13:8

- "Above all, love *each other* deeply, because love covers over a multitude of sins." —1 Peter 4:8

ACCEPTANCE

- "Be at peace with *each other*."
  —Mark 9:50

- "Live in harmony with *one another*." —Romans 12:16

- "Let us stop passing judgment on *one another*." —Romans 14:13

- "Accept *one another*, then, just as Christ accepted you, in order to bring praise to God."
  —Romans 15:7

ENCOURAGEMENT

- "And so we will be with the Lord forever. Therefore encourage *each other* with these words."
—1 Thessalonians 4:17–18

- "And let us consider how we can spur *one another* on towards love and good deeds." —Hebrews 10:24

- "He died for us so that whether we are awake or asleep, we may live together with him. Therefore, encourage *one another* and build *each other* up." —1 Thessalonians 5:10–11

- "Let us . . . not give up meeting together, as some are in the habit of doing, but let us encourage *one another*." —Hebrews 10:24–25

CARING

- "Serve *one another* humbly in love." —Galatians 5:13

- "Carry *each other's* burdens." —Galatians 6:2

- "Honor *one another* above yourselves." —Romans 12:10

- "Confess your sins to *each other* and pray for *each other*." —James 5:16

- "Be kind and compassionate to *one another*." —Ephesians 4:32

AFFECTION

Three times in the New Testament Paul encourages the Christ followers to "greet *one another* with a holy kiss" (Romans 16:16, 1 Corinthians 16:20, and 2 Corinthians 13:12). In our twenty-first century, a kiss would certainly raise eyebrows and potentially get you in trouble. Recently, a TV newscaster referred to churches as a place where hugs and handshakes are in abundance. What a great testimony! Therefore, we should be people who freely demonstrate our love toward *one another* in an acceptable manner.

INSTRUCTION

- "Instruct *one another*."
  —Romans 15:14

- "Wash *one another's* feet."
  —John 13:14

- "Be filled with the Spirit, speaking to *one another* with psalms, hymns, and songs from the Spirit."
  —Ephesians 5:18–19

- "Teach and admonish *one another* with all wisdom." —Colossians 3:16

If we take our cues from our often self-obsessed culture, finding purpose in retirement will be challenging, if not impossible. Just imagine the influence each of us could have by practicing the "one anothers" within our sphere of influence, even if that's just a few people. They can be practiced through every stage of retirement regardless of age or declining health. The "one anothers" are all about mirroring Christ, giving yourself away, being an encourager, and demonstrating loving relationships. You can even practice that on your deathbed.

(Note from Bill: It's worth pointing out that Bob was the epitome of this during his last days. He engaged with people, encouraged those around him, shared deep wisdom, and as his body weakened, lived with a strength of character that was truly inspiring.)

I was particularly convicted by biblical instructions about encouragement because I was so aware of how powerful encouraging words had been in my life. On the other hand, discouraging words, particularly from people we are closest to, can have such a devastating impact. I resolved to ask for God's direction as I sought opportunities to encourage others on a regular basis. My goal was to be true to God's injunction to live out the "one anothers" while trusting Him with the results. I found many opportunities to live this out in the years after I fully retired—and even more so after I received a terminal cancer diagnosis.

IN GOD'S SUFFICIENCY

When I knew the end of my life was fast approaching, I had a conversation with my friend Bill, with whom I had discussed some of my thoughts on retirement. I had been blessed to be part of a church community group that had come alongside Nancy and me as we faced this phase of our lives together. Bill and his wife were part of that group and had become our dear friends.

Bill mentioned how my example of acceptance, realistic optimism, and faith had come up in a recent conversation with his brother. They were discussing some challenging issues in their personal lives when Bill decided to share my story. Bill told me this put things in perspective for them both.

First, Bill and his brother realized that compared to my current situation, the issues they were dealing with seemed meaningless. And second, they agreed that if they followed my example as they dealt with their "stuff," everything would work out just fine. Bill mentioned how interesting it was that I had so powerfully impacted his brother, someone I didn't even know. This was simply an example of what I call *dynamic purpose in God's sufficiency*. Bill seemed to like that term and asked me to elaborate.

I told him that God's dynamic purpose is powerful and real, but it can be hard to define. It's unseen and we are rarely aware of it as it happens. God's dynamic purpose is always working for good, and it often grows exponentially into the lives of those far outside our circle of influence. My impact on Bill's brother would be a good example.

As my thoughts turned to other examples of God's dynamic purpose in my life, I told Bill about my troubled childhood full of uncertainty and abuse. But I think the suffering I endured in childhood enabled me to arrive at Jesus's feet. That, too, was an example of God's dynamic purpose. Sometimes we see things more clearly as the result of suffering.

I view retirement, including dealing with end-of-life issues, as a conduit for God's dynamic purpose. Although I know I am not perfect in this regard, I realize God has already used me for good in the lives of others. I'm not

Sometimes we see things more clearly as the result of suffering.

capable of that on my own. That's where "God's sufficiency" comes in. It's only through God that we can do anything of real value. This is why the credit (or glory, if you prefer) should go to Him.

Due to our propensity for pride, God doesn't always show us how or when he's working in and through us. Our attitude should be one of humility. As C. S. Lewis said in Mere Christianity, "We have only been shown the plan insofar as it concerns ourselves"—and that should be just fine with us.

Dynamic purpose in God's sufficiency has been at work in every stage of my life. When I was quite young, my cousins told me that even though I rarely spoke, they thought that I would become a pastor one day because I "cared so much for people."

I also remember a boss early in my career who, even though I was reserved and self-conscious, promoted me to an outside sales position because "people trust you." Those seemingly innocuous comments had a lifelong impact on me. They gave me vision and confidence that I otherwise would not have developed. I found success both in the pastoral and business worlds as my life unfolded, although I couldn't have predicted my success in either of those spheres. Most of the time we don't know what God is doing while He's doing it. And we often see things more clearly in the rearview mirror.

Sometimes, though, you don't have to look too hard. For example, my family recently took me on a beach vacation. My biggest concern at the time was that Nancy would be cared for after I was gone. As that trip unfolded, it was clear to me that this was exactly what God was showing me during our time at the beach. Surrounded by the love and community of our family, I knew she would be well taken care of when I departed. No words can begin to convey that comfort. Now that's dynamic purpose in God's sufficiency. I think my purpose now, as I face the end of my life, is to reflect His sufficiency to those who cross my path. I have no idea how this will work or come to pass . . . but I trust that it will.

CHAPTER 4

GOD'S PROVISION

And my God will meet all your needs according
to the riches of his glory in Christ Jesus.
—Philippians 4:19

When I was born, I had trouble breathing and almost died. Doctors placed me in an iron lung to help my lungs develop. I continued to be very sickly throughout my childhood, and my older brother and I suffered verbal and sometimes physical abuse at the hands of our mother. But even in the face of major physical and psychological challenges as I grew up, I knew in my heart that God was providing for me. My brother and I both experienced God as "our refuge and strength, an ever-present help in trouble" (Psalm 46:1). God's provision was woven throughout our whole lives in the form of our father.

In the 1940s, my dad was a day laborer earning less than minimum wage. But somehow, he would often come home with a Baby Ruth chocolate bar for my brother and a box of Good and Plenty licorice candy for me, which he knew were our favorites. I've never forgotten the joy on my dad's face as he watched us eat that candy. It was a seemingly small gesture but one that has resonated with me my entire life. Not only was it indicative of how much our father loved us, but it also was an example of God's provision amid the challenges we were facing.

This is why I'm so passionate about the "one anothers" of the Bible and the influence we might have in the lives of those around us—if we simply act out of love like my dad did. He didn't fully realize the impact he was having on me with that candy, but his kindness has stayed with me ever since. This, I believe, was God's way of providing for my brother and me. Dad's job was to act out of love; the results were from and through God's hands.

WILLING TO ACCEPT

Being aware of God's provision is essential if we are to make sense of life during the stage of retirement in which we start to experience losses—loss of spouse, friends, family, health, physical stamina, or mental acuity. The key is to acknowledge that He is in control, He is God even when we don't understand, and He provides if we are willing to accept whatever circumstances life brings. We often have trouble comprehending things in life like abuse, suffering, evil, and death. We sometimes struggle with faith. However, as we learn to trust in Him, the gift of His presence becomes our most valued possession.

When you receive any gift, regardless of the giver's intention, the recipient must have a receptive and grateful spirit to appreciate it. We often receive gifts that we never use after we open them. Other gifts we cherish for the rest of our lives. The key variable is in the heart of the person on the receiving end. Spiritually, this is all tied to our faith in and reverence for God.

Some things we simply won't understand this side of heaven, and "bad" things can and will happen. But, as C. S. Lewis says in *Mere Christianity*, "This is near the stage where the road passes over the rim of the world." I take comfort in knowing that if I am willing to acknowledge God in all my ways, He will direct my paths (to paraphrase Proverbs 3:6). This applies at every stage of life . . . particularly toward the end.

We often receive gifts that we never use after we open them. Other gifts we cherish for the rest of our lives. The key variable is in the heart of the person on the receiving end.

Since I am writing this during the hospice stage of my life, I can tell you that near the end, adversity can blindside you unless you have some warning. It can be all-encompassing when all you can do is eat, sleep, and go to the bathroom. However, the question I ask myself is, *How do I get from "oh, poor me" to "this is great"?*

When I go to sleep, I try to remember to give thanks for the day without qualifying my gratitude with "buts" and "whys," and I pray that "His will, not mine" be done. When I wake up, I'm grateful for quiet time in the mornings so I can ease into the day. Sometimes, though, it's difficult. On certain days, I must simply choose to say, "This is the day the Lord has made, and I will . . . damn it . . . make the best of it."

I've come to realize that this stage of my life is truly a gift from God. I'm so grateful for the time with my family and friends, particularly time with my wife, Nancy. I can honestly say that in sixty-two years of marriage, this—*right now*—is the best time of all. And none of it would have happened without the challenges brought about by cancer and the resulting terminal diagnosis. I know this may sound crazy to some people. Sometimes, though, it's best to think of the trials of life as a gift . . . because, I believe, they are.

The challenges I'm facing enable me to see, with more clarity than ever, the meaning of James 1:2–4: "Consider it pure joy, my brothers and sisters, whenever you face trials of many kinds, because you know that the testing of your faith produces perseverance. Let perseverance finish its work so that you may be mature and complete, *not lacking anything*" (italics mine).

Trials enable you to become aware of God's presence more acutely and to grow spiritually in unexpected ways. Adversity provides a window to God's sufficiency. Trials and adversity open the door to tangibly feel the love of Christ, and are often the mechanism through which God works in our lives. There can be no greater gifts than these.

FINDING JOY

The awareness of God's presence in all circumstances and acknowledging Him in all my ways have led to a real sense of joy in my life, even as I face its conclusion. I may not always feel happy, but I can choose to live with a joyful perspective.

Happiness is like joy, but more *in the moment*. It is a feeling of accomplishment at the conclusion of a task. It's the belly laugh while listening to a hilarious story. It's a good meal with friends or family. It's leaving a show or movie with a smile. It's winning a game. It's making a new friend. These are all beautiful moments, but they can be fleeting, they come and go.

Joy is deeper than happiness. It's more a *state of being* than a one-time event. Joy is a sense of contentment despite circumstances. It's a mindset that seeks to learn wisdom from mistakes, trials, and disappointments. It's one of the benefits of old age as we realize that God has seen us through the bad times; therefore, we can face each new day with joy.

Recently, I was sitting around the table with my granddaughter, her boyfriend, and my grandson. The discussion was about attaining wealth. Suddenly my grandson piped up and said, "Attaining wealth is very simple—you determine how much you are going to give away, save 10 percent, and learn to live on what is left." I was pleased to hear that some of what I'd taught him had stuck. As any parent knows, when we impart advice to our kids we rarely know if they're listening to what we say.

I managed to keep my mouth shut and bask in the inward joy I felt at that moment; I had no need to elaborate. Joy is when you know that your adult child or grandchild has internalized the wisdom you've tried to instill and made it their own. Joy builds over a lifetime of relationships and experiences—if we look for it, cultivate it, and seek God amid whatever circumstance or stage of life we're in.

The Bible has much to say about joy. Here are some verses that relate to this theme:

- "You make known to me the path of life; you will fill me with joy in your presence." —Psalm 16:11

- "Do not grieve, for the joy of the Lord is your strength."
  —Nehemiah 8:10

- "You turned my wailing into dancing, you removed my sackcloth and clothed me with joy."
  —Psalm 30:11

- "Your statutes are my heritage forever; they are the joy of my heart." —Psalm 119:111

- "They will enter Zion with singing; everlasting joy will crown their heads. Gladness and joy will overtake them, and sorrow and sighing will flee away."
  —Isaiah 35:10

- "I have told you this so that my joy may be in you and that your joy may be complete."
  —John 15:11

Regardless of our circumstances in life, good or bad, the key to a joyful spirit is having an awareness of God's presence and trust in His provision. When I've found this challenging, I've found it helpful to look back on the times in my life where I know God directed my path. That's what I believe Charles Spurgeon meant with the "rule of three" I mentioned earlier. He has provided, He is providing, and He will provide. Therefore, I have confidence for the days to come and in eternity with Him, even if I don't know exactly what that may look like.

CHAPTER 5

NEW HOME

For we know that if the earthly tent
we live in is destroyed, we have a
building from God, an eternal house in
heaven, not built by human hands.
—2 Corinthians 5:1

On February 7, 1990, I lost the most positive influence in my life. At 5:30 that morning, I received the phone call I had prayed would not come for at least another five hours. Five hours would have at least given me time to return to the nursing home to be with my father in his last moments. The previous evening, my mother and I were visiting him when she had demanded that I take her home. I gave in and have regretted that decision ever since. We had been told his life expectancy was less than two weeks, but now he was gone. My dad deserved more than to die alone.

Two weeks earlier, I'd had the difficult task of informing my father that the medical staff could do nothing more for him and he needed to be moved to a nursing home. I was trying to tell him this when he raised his hand, which was his way of conveying that he wanted to speak. In his halting, labored speech, he said, "Now, Bob, I know that my time is up, but I have had a good life. I have faith and it's okay."

Internally, I wanted to scream. I just didn't want to accept the reality of his death. But my dad had a different perspective that was, and is, superior. He modeled acceptance, gratitude, deep faith, and contentment at the end of his life. He finished well, and I'd like to do the same. However, these qualities can be hard to attain and aren't always evident as people face the end of their lives.

He modeled acceptance, gratitude, deep faith, and contentment at the end of his life. He finished well, and I'd like to do the same.

NOTE FROM BILL

Bob never finished the rest of this chapter relating to eternal perspective. He told me he hadn't written any of the content down, but that was okay. "It's all in my head," he said. I figured Bob would likely have much to say on the topic, particularly considering his terminal illness, and I wanted to hear his thoughts.

The next time we got together, Bob and I sat next to each other in large, identical recliners in his living room. Looking small and frail, Bob sank deep in his chair, his voice raspy from the effects of cancer treatments. His mind tended to wander, so I recorded what he was saying in hopes of gleaning as much as I could from our time together.

When I prompted him about Heaven, things got interesting. He had more to say on this topic than anything else we'd covered when talking about the book. His thoughts were among the richest pieces of wisdom he had ever shared with me, which is saying a lot. But sometimes, due to his condition, his train of thought seemed disjointed, and I had trouble following. I realized later as I reviewed the recording that he was communicating on a level beyond my understanding. I think that's because when we get closer to death, we start to see things that others can't yet see. He was connected to something deeper. Nevertheless, I found his comments, quoted below, powerful—to say the least.

OBITUARIES AND PRAYER REQUESTS

The first thing Bob mentioned when I asked him about Heaven was that he was "rebelling against the obituary because a

Christian has eternal life, and an obituary implies that this is the end." His life ending on earth simply meant that he was passing from one life to the next. Death marked a new beginning, one much longer and more significant than anything he had previously experienced. Therefore, what some would call a funeral, he called a "celebration of life." What some would call an obituary, he called "Bob's story." His story would have to mention that he had "entered into the presence of his Savior." Those phrases were all consistent with Bob's perspective on life, his belief in the reality of Heaven, and his concept of what Heaven is like.

Another thing I found interesting was that Bob wasn't particularly enamored with the idea of prayer requests. He said, "It's okay to ask for your daily bread, but it's more about what God is doing—His kingdom come; His will be done." And the key was to focus on the "sufficiency of God." For example, Bob's voice was affected significantly from cancer and he was often hard to understand. He admitted this was frustrating. "When I feel like saying I want my voice back, I repent of that and say it's all about God." Instead of praying for the return of his voice, he redirected his thoughts and prayers toward an eternal perspective, acceptance of his present circumstance, and trust in God's sufficiency. I couldn't help but wonder if I could do the same as I dealt with the less dramatic issues of my daily life—or if one day I were in circumstances like Bob's.

NEEDING NOTHING

Bob's concept of Heaven was that it was "not about emerald streets but rather about being face-to-face with Christ and sitting at His feet. And if Christ is there, what more do you need?" He said he thought of this often "when he couldn't sleep or when he saw Nancy in pain." As he faced those challenges, and many others brought about by his cancer, he looked forward to Christ's presence in Heaven. He also believed that he was in Christ's presence every moment of his earthly life. "If you want to get through the Christian life, you have to say, 'God is there.'" That belief was what accounted for how well Bob lived his life—emotionally, mentally, and spiritually. It's also why he had so much impact on the people around him, including myself, in those final days.

SEEING CLEARLY

As our conversation that evening came to an end, Bob mentioned that to him, the "Christian life is all about God and relationships" (loving God, loving others) and action. "It's about what you do"—for example, getting up in the morning and studying Scriptures (or whatever else you believe God is calling you to do). But it "isn't about us declaring our own godliness"—looking for credit, living for yourself, or trying to live on your own power.

We discussed Bob's belief that Heaven is about seeing things more clearly, like looking through a clean window on a sunny day. He said, "When you get to Heaven, you are going to say, oh . . . I get it now . . . but I could be wrong . . . and that's okay." Bob didn't need to see with total clarity this side of Heaven. He believed that whatever happened would ultimately be good, because he would be face-to-face with Jesus Christ. This reminded us both of a Bible verse, but neither of us could recall it at the time, so I looked it up. "For now we see only a reflection as in a mirror; then we shall see face to face. Now I know in part; then I shall know fully, even as I am fully known" (1 Corinthians 13:12). There was not much more we could add to that, so we thought it best to leave it there.

Months after Bob had passed, I ran across a passage in a Bible commentary by William Barclay that read,

---

If we really grasped the truth of the Christian faith, we would always be glad when those whom we love go to be with God. That is not to say that we would not feel the sting of sorrow and the sharpness of loss; but even in our sorrow and loneli-ness, we would be glad that after

the troubles and the trials of earth those whom we loved have gone to something better. We would never grudge them their rest but would remember that they had entered, not into death, but into blessedness.

I think Bob Little would have agreed.

EPILOGUE

What we alone can do we cannot do alone.
—*Martin Laird*

A s I (Bill) come to the end of this project, the cliché "God works in mysterious ways" comes to mind. I've been unable to find that exact phrase in the Bible. Nevertheless, I think it applies here perfectly. When I started putting this book together, my intent was simply to share Bob's thoughts about retirement. This made sense based on my relationship with him, our common writing interest, and the timing of events in both of our lives.

As it turned out, preparing this book coincided with my own journey into "retirement," and I have been blessed by Bob's wisdom in ways I never could have imagined. As I pored over Bob's source material, I was often struck with the feeling that God was speaking to me through Bob's words, thoughts, and example. I didn't see any of this coming when I first started talking to Bob about his book many years ago. This is an example of the mysterious ways in which God works—how little we see in the moment, how important it is to trust in Him, and how good He is to us. And this all ties in with Bob's concept of dynamic purpose in God's sufficiency. God is always at work for good in our circumstances, regardless of how mundane or dramatic, but this is often hidden from our immediate awareness.

To use Bob's words, "God is in control, and He provides if we are willing to accept that He is God, even when we don't get it."

CIRCLING AROUND

When Bob was first explaining the concepts behind this book, he said that the first four stages of biblically-based retirement could be called "God's grace." I didn't quite understand what he meant until a few weeks later when I was reading a book called *The Divine Conspiracy* by Dallas Willard. In it, Willard defines grace as "God's doing for us what we can't do for ourselves." We don't have the ability to understand or live out the

"God is in control, and He provides if we are willing to accept that He is God, even when we don't get it."

first four stages of retirement without God providing us the ability. We must rely on God's grace. To use another quote from Willard, "Saints (people of faith) burn grace like a jet burns fuel at takeoff." They need lots of grace because they are relying on God to enable them to do things far beyond their human capacities (Bob was a great example of that).

Bob pointed out that in the last stage of retirement, which he called Heaven, we won't need God's grace anymore—because we are already living in it. Comments like that tended to make me stop and think. I'm still working that one out.

Another insight was that the first four stages are not chronological; instead, they intertwine and overlap, or in Bob's words, "Things sort of circle around." At the core of each stage is dynamic purpose in God's sufficiency. And Heaven, listed as the last of the stages, is truly another new beginning.

Clearly Bob believed that. His faith pointed him toward a power and purpose higher than himself, that impacted how he lived at every stage of retirement. He didn't have to understand how it all would come together. He just needed to keep his ears and eyes open to God's voice and direction. Understanding would come once he got to Heaven where, he believed, being in God's presence would be all that mattered anyway.

Fortunately, the impact Bob made during his earthly life would still be felt—and be very real—in the lives of those he left behind. For those impacted by Bob's life, like me, that makes us very fortunate indeed.

CLEAN WINDOWS

Bob modeled his faith in several ways. The first was *acceptance*. He didn't spend much time, if any, bemoaning his fate. While he admitted that he didn't always like what was happening, he accepted his circumstance as he trusted in God's provision and grace.

Another was his *realistic optimism*. He said that sometimes you must choose between bitterness and faith; obviously, he chose faith. Amid his mental and physical decline, he was determined to praise God and make the most of each day despite his circumstances. He was open about his fears, frustrations, and disappointments. But he did so with a spirit of unwavering hope and optimism.

Considering his terminal cancer diagnosis, Bob realized that this perspective might be hard for some people to understand. Sometimes, I think, it was hard even for him to explain. Bob often said when referring to his positive attitude, "I don't think I'm in denial." He was aware of the reality and finality of his prognosis, but his spirit was rooted in an eternal perspective that enabled him to be optimistic anyway.

What stood out most for me was Bob's *humility*. He knew he was an inspiration to people during his final days but still seemed perplexed by it. He believed that God's dynamic purpose was usually hidden from our immediate awareness or understanding—and that this was by God's design. If we fully understood the good God was doing through us, then we'd be tempted to take the credit. We are hardwired for pride, which is why God only shows us things on a "need-to-know basis."

This, I think, explains why Bob was so humble when he received compliments from people. He truly didn't see how much positive impact he was having because he wasn't meant to. Bob's humility was based on his belief that whatever good came *through him* was provided *to him*. To borrow a line from Thomas Merton in *New Seeds of Contemplation*, "The humble man receives praise the way a clean window takes the light of the sun. The truer and more intense the light is, the less you see of the glass." Personally, I think Bob's window was pretty clean.

SPIRITUAL FUNDAMENTALS

I once got to see Michael Jordan play basketball from courtside seats. When I had watched basketball on TV, the cameras followed Jordan everywhere. His occasional spectacular dunks were replayed over and over. But in person he didn't seem all that impressive. Jordan looked pretty much like the other nine guys running up and down the court.

However, when I looked up at the scoreboard, Michael Jordan was always the guy scoring the most points. I think that's because he was focused on making the routine plays. And he rarely, if ever, made mistakes. This, I submit, is what really set him apart from the other players. Jordan was more fundamentally sound than his peers and didn't call attention to himself, whether he was making a routine assist or rising above the basket for a dunk. His success was the result of endless repetition, unwavering focus, and total commitment.

This sports analogy, I think, reflects Bob's spirituality and approach to life. Just like a great athlete, he was all about the fundamentals rooted in his faith. And he stayed focused consistently throughout his whole life. I know Bob would say he made mistakes along the way, which, I suppose, is true. However, like Michael Jordan playing basketball, any mistakes he made were rare and imperceptible to those watching from the sidelines.

Bob achieved a lot professionally, but the real impact he made was on the lives of other people. He often said he believed that his purpose in retirement was to model how to grow old gracefully and how to die well—in that respect, his execution was spectacular. I know, however, that he wouldn't attribute that to his own spiritual prowess but instead to God's leading and direction, His Spirit, and His sovereignty. I suppose that's fair enough considering Bob's spiritual perspective.

My hope is that I can follow Bob's example and execute the fundamentals of faith as well as he did. It was a privilege and a blessing to watch him live out his purpose from a courtside seat.

—Bill Schillings

APPENDIX

THE GOSPEL OF BOB

Buried in one of Bob's computer files, I (Bill) found the following material I thought worth including here. I've entitled it "The Gospel of Bob" because it encapsulates many of the principles in this book, exemplifies how integrated the Bible was to Bob's thinking, and summarizes the "good news" on which he based his life.

I looked up the versions of the Bible he referred to in this piece of writing and determined that he used six different translations when compiling the verses. But I attributed two of the verses to the BLT (Bob Little Translation), because I couldn't find an exact match for them in any translation.[1] Those verses, I assume, Bob wrote from memory based on his reading of the other translations. Clearly, this was a man who loved the Bible and was relentless in his search for the meaning and nuance of the text.

SPIRITUAL ALIVENESS
—BY BOB LITTLE

Look upon yourselves as "alive to God through Christ Jesus our Lord."[2] In our later years, when we aren't quite the physical specimens of strength we once were, how easy it can be sometimes to feel nearly drained of life itself. That's why it's so important, as we grow older, to keep embracing the basic truths of our dynamic aliveness in Christ. Through faith in Christ, we now are alive to God, alert to him, through Jesus Christ our Lord. We have become "alive to all that is good."[3] All your spiritual aliveness is drawn from the life of Christ Himself, "the author of life."[4] By believing in Jesus, you "have already passed from death into life."[5] Our sense of aliveness is bonded with the One who proclaims Himself as "the way and the truth and the life."[6]

Jesus closely identifies your life with Himself. He says, "I am the resurrection and the life. Whoever believes in me, though he die, yet shall he live."[7] He continues,

"Because I live, you also will live."[8] And He promises, "For as the Father raises the dead and gives them life, so also the Son gives life to whom he will."[9]

Now that you and I have received "this wildly extravagant life-gift,"[10] it's our vital and daily privilege to see "the life of Jesus . . . manifested in our bodies"[11] so that we "might live to God"[12] rather than living selfishly. "Instead, give yourselves completely to God, for you were dead, but now you have new life. So use your whole body as an instrument to do what is right for the glory of God."[13] Remember this instruction: "Since you have been raised to new life with Christ, *set your sights on the realities of heaven*, where Christ sits in the place of honor at God's right hand."[14] Finally, "Apply your mind to things above not to things on earth."[15]

We're to keep coming to the Scriptures and nurturing our minds with the truth we find there. Jesus promises, "Whoever continues to feed on Me (whoever takes Me for his food and is nourished by Me) shall, in his turn, live through and because of Me."[16]

1 NKJV—New King James Version; PH—Phillips New Testament in Modern English; NLT—New Living Translation; NIV—New International Version; ESV—English Standard Version; MSG—The Message; BLT—Bob Little Translation.

2 Romans 6:11 NKJV.

3 1 Peter 2:24 PH.

4 Acts 3:15 NLT.

5 John 5:24 NLT.

6 John 14:6 NIV.

7 John 11:25 ESV.

8 John 14:19 NIV.

9 John 5:12 ESV.

10 Romans 5:17 MSG.

11 2 Corinthians 4:10 ESV.

12 Galatians 2:19 ESV.

13 Romans 6:13 NLT.

14 Colossians 3:1 NLT.

15 Colossians 3:2 BLT.

16 John 6:57 BLT.

BOB'S REMEMBRANCE

Delivered by Bill Schillings
June 25, 2022

Two months ago, I was in a shoe store shopping for some running shoes. My phone rang. It was Bob Little. He was planning this memorial service and wondered if I'd be willing to speak at it.

Initially, I couldn't get words to come out of my mouth. I felt tears in my eyes as I tried to compose myself. Finally, I blurted out something like . . . "Yeah, Bob, I'd be honored to do that." Bob mentioned how grateful he was that in his illness he had been given time to plan and to spend time with his family. He said that in over sixty years of marriage to Nancy, this had been the best time of all. Again, I found myself kind of dumbfounded. I remember saying, "Well, Bob, God is good."

His response was, and these were his exact words: "God is incredibly good."

I think that sums up what Bob would want us to take away from this service.

He said his desire was that people wouldn't blather on too long. And, most importantly, that whatever was said should direct people's attention to God's glory rather than Bob's accomplishments. As our conversation ended, he said, almost apologetically, that he didn't know when this service was going to be. Apparently, he felt this might be some sort of imposition on my time. Well, Bob, if you're listening, I can assure you there is nothing I'd rather be doing than talking about you right now.

God's power flowed through Bob Little like water through a mountain creek after a rainstorm. But this came so naturally to him that he often seemed unaware of it. If you said to him, "Hey, Bob, what you just said was really wise," or "What you did really impacted me," he would often look kind of perplexed, as if he couldn't figure out why you thought this might be attributable to him. He had this unique combination of deep wisdom, abiding faith, and genuine humility. I've been trying to think of one word that sums this up. But words sometimes have their limits. Maybe that's why that mountain creek metaphor keeps coming back into my head.

Bob knew that the power of the stream only comes from the rain that God provides. He was simply a willing channel through which the water flowed. In Christian circles we have terms for this: walking with Jesus, being aware of God's presence, surrendering to His will, or having a mind controlled by the Spirit. Whatever you want to call it, Bob Little epitomized it.

So, at the risk of "blathering on," I'll give you a few quick illustrations of what I'm talking about. Sometime last fall, our community group was trying to close for the evening, but we were struggling to come to some conclusion for our discussion. As usual, Bob had been quiet, quite content to let others talk. Fortunately, someone had the bright idea to ask, "So, Bob, what do you think?"

What followed from Bob was a summary full of deep insight, wise observations, and practical application for our lives. When he finished, there was a pregnant pause. No one knew what to say next. So Diane

Lutfy, bless her heart, turns to Bob, looks him in the eye, and says, "You know, Bob, you are a very wise person . . . you are like our Yoda." As was typical, Bob looked somewhat puzzled.

Fast-forward to last March, when Bob, Nancy, and Fred and JC Dwiggins were over at my house for lunch. Everyone came over at 1 p.m. Three hours later, it was just me, Fred, and Bob sitting at the dining room table. The conversation had turned to transitions in life and a book Bob had been working on about retirement. What he was saying was blowing us away.

I detached from the conversation for just a moment. I glanced over at Freddy. He was literally sitting on the edge of his seat, leaning forward, fully engaged in what Bob was saying. I realized I was in the exact same position. Here was a dying man in his eighties holding two grown men in their sixties in rapt attention as he shared his thoughts on the meaning of life and how to live it well. I wished we could have sat there until dinner. Bob, no doubt, was unaware of his Yoda-like status in our eyes.

Last month, I had a chance to spend a few more precious moments in conversation with Bob. I mentioned how much impact he and Nancy were having on other people, even people they didn't know. He said, "Oh, that's just an example of dynamic purpose in God's sufficiency." Needless to say, I asked him to elaborate.

He said, "Well, it's all about the "one anothers." He explained that the New Testament refers to the "one anothers" fifty-eight times. He had organized them into six categories: love one another, accept one another, encourage one another, serve one another, show affection for one another, and instruct one another. After he told me this, he paused briefly, as if to give me an example, and said, "Bill, I admire your mind. I admire who you are." Especially considering the source, I think that's possibly the single most encouraging thing anyone has ever said to me—that was dynamic purpose in God's sufficiency.

And on that Yoda moment, maybe it's best I bring this to a close. And even though I wish I could experience a few more of them in Bob's presence, I think the ones I had will do for quite some time. What a blessing Bob Little was, and is, in my life. And I'm certain that everyone touched by his life, particularly the people in this room, feel the same way.

God is good. No, wait, check that—God is *incredibly good*. Thanks, Bob.

REFERENCE LIST

Barclay, William. *The New Bible Study Commentary Series*. Louisville: Westminster John Knox Press, 2017.

Brooks, David. *The Road to Character.* New York: Random House, 2015.

Hall, Robert, ed. *Charles Spurgeon: The Power of Prayer in a Believer's Life.* Seattle: YWAM Publishing, 1996.

Lewis, C. S. *Mere Christianity.* London: Geoffrey Bles, 1952.

Merton, Thomas. *New Seeds of Contemplation.* New York: New Directions, 1972.

Willard, Dallas. *The Divine Conspiracy: Rediscovering Our Hidden Life in God.* New York: Harper Publishing, 1998.